ACKNOWLEDGEMENTS

Publishing Director	Piers Pickard
Publisher	Tim Cook
Commissioning Editor	Jen Feroze
Illustrators	Andy Mansfield
	Sebastien Iwohn
Designer	Andy Mansfield
Print production	Larissa Frost,
	Nigel Longuet

Published in March 2017 by Lonely Planet Global Ltd
CRN: 554153
ISBN: 978 1 78657 316 2
www.lonelyplanetkids.com
© Lonely Planet 2017
Printed in China

10 9 8 7 6 5 4 3 2 1

Lonely Planet Offices

AUSTRALIA
The Malt Store, Level 3, 551 Swanston St,
Carlton, Victoria 3053
T: 03 8379 8000

IRELAND
Unit E, Digital Court, The Digital Hub,
Rainsford St, Dublin 8

USA
124 Linden St, Oakland, CA 94607
T: 510 250 6400

UK
240 Blackfriars Rd, London SE1 8NW
T: 020 3771 5100

STAY IN TOUCH lonelyplanet.com/contact

first words
SPANISH

Illustrated by
Andy Mansfield & Sebastien Iwohn

hello

---

hola

(oh-lah)

ice cream

helado

(eh-lah-doh)

water

---

agua

(a-gwa)

supermarket
supermercado
(soo-pair-mair-kah-doh)

trolley
carrito
(ka-ree-toh)

cat

---

gato

(ga-toh)

bus
autobús
(ow-toh-boos)

dress
---
vestido

(ves-tee-doh)

dog

perro

(peh-roh)

$$\frac{\text{banana}}{\text{plátano}}$$

(pla-ta-noh)

carrot
---
zanahoria

(za-na-or-ree-ya)

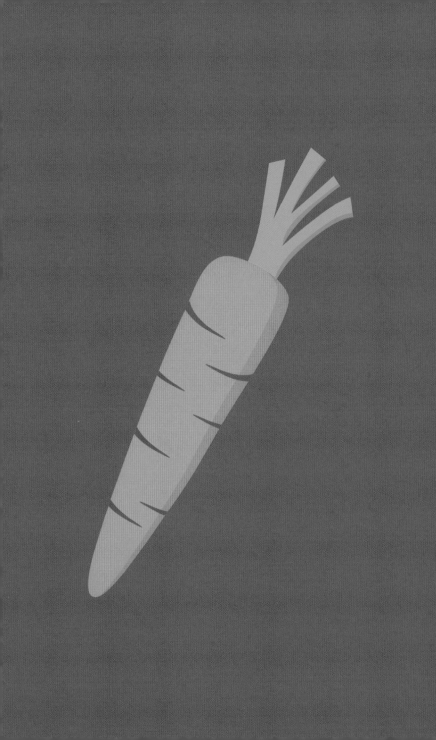

taxi
taxi

(tak-see)

t-shirt
camiseta
(ka-mee-seh-ta)

fish
---
pescado

(pes-kah-doh)

aeroplane
avión

(av-ee-on)

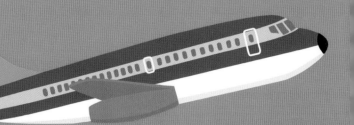

horse

caballo

(ka-ba-yo)

french fries
---
patatas fritas

(pa-ta-tas free-tas)

swimming pool
piscina
(pee-see-na)

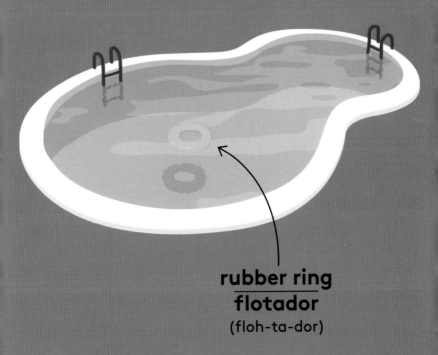

rubber ring
flotador
(floh-ta-dor)

cheese
_____
queso
(keh-soh)

towel
toalla
(toh-al-ya)

doctor

doctor/doctora

(dok-tor/dok-tora)

apple

manzana

(man-za-na)

worm
gusano
(goo-sa-noh)

beach
---
playa

(pla-ya)

bicycle
bicicleta
(bee-see-kle-ta)

airport

aeropuerto

(aye-roh-pwair-toh)

juice

---

jugo

(khoo-go)

bakery
panadería
(pa-na-de-ree-a)

shoes
---
zapatos

(za-pa-tos)

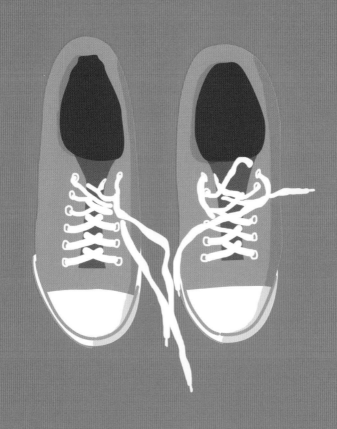

phone
teléfono

(te-leh-fo-noh)

post office
correos
(ko-ray-os)

restaurant
---
restaurante

(res-tow-ran-teh)

hotel
hotel

(oh-tel)

milk
---
leche

(leh-tchay)

chocolate
chocolate

(tcho-koh-lah-teh)

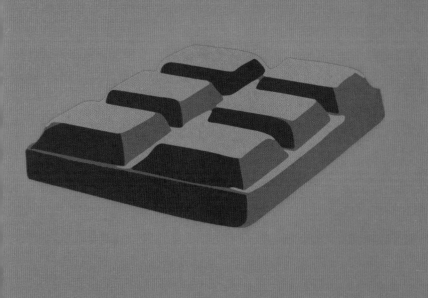

car
---
coche

(ko-tchay)

hat
sombrero

(som-brair-roh)

sunglasses
gafas de sol

(ga-fas dey sol)

chicken

pollo

(pol-yo)

train
tren

(tren)

station
estación
(es-ta-see-on)

clock

reloj

(re-lokh)

toilet
---
servicio

(sair-vee-see-oh)

bed

---

cama

(ka-ma)

house
---
casa

(ka-sa)

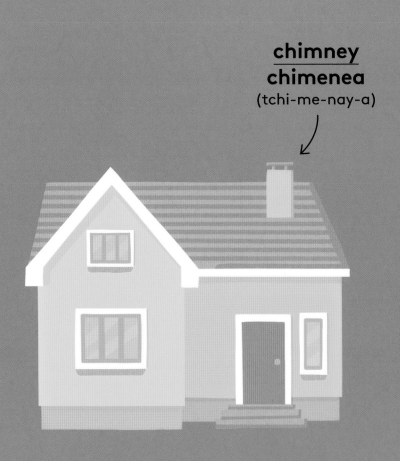

chimney
chimenea
(tchi-me-nay-a)

trousers

pantalones

(pan-ta-loh-nes)

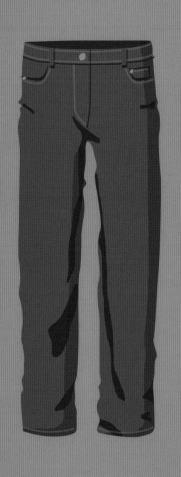

suitcase
---
maleta

(ma-leh-ta)

plate
plato
(pla-toh)

knife
cuchillo
(koo-tchee-lyo)

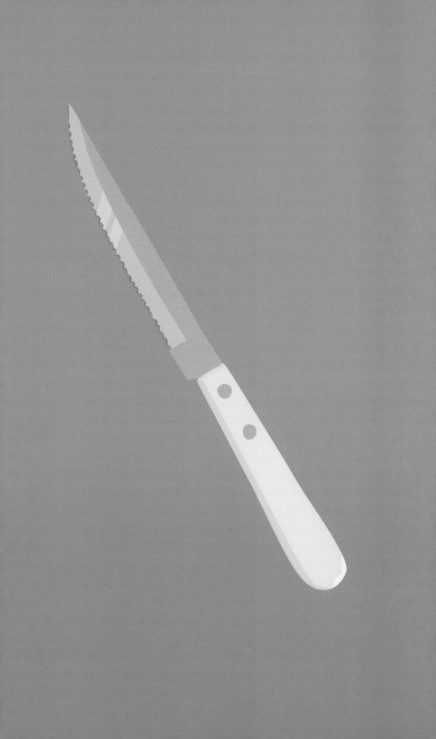

fork

---

tenedor

(teh-nay-dor)

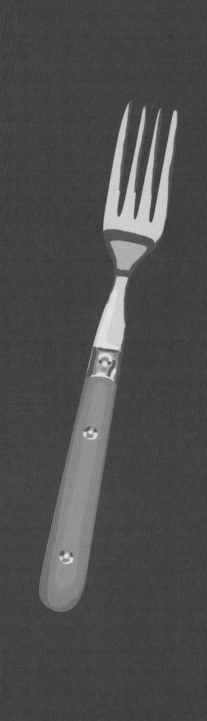

spoon
---
cuchara

(koo-tcha-ra)

computer
ordenador

(or-day-na-dor)

mouse
ratón
(ra-ton)

book
libro
(lee-broh)

sandwich
---
emparedado

(em-pa-reh-dah-doh)

yes

sí

(see)

no
no
(no)

cinema

---

cine

(see-nay)

park

parque

(par-keh)

menu
---
menú

(meh-noo)

passport

pasaporte

(pas-a-por-teh)

police officer
policía
(po-lee-see-a)

key
llave
(lya-vay)

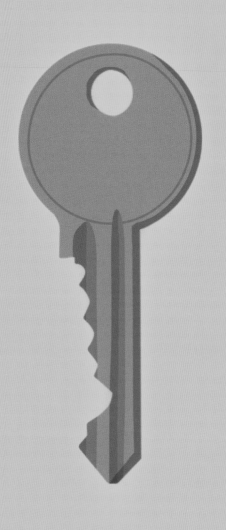

ticket
---
boleto

(bo-leh-toh)

pineapple
piña
(pee-nya)

rain
lluvia

(lyoo-vee-ah)

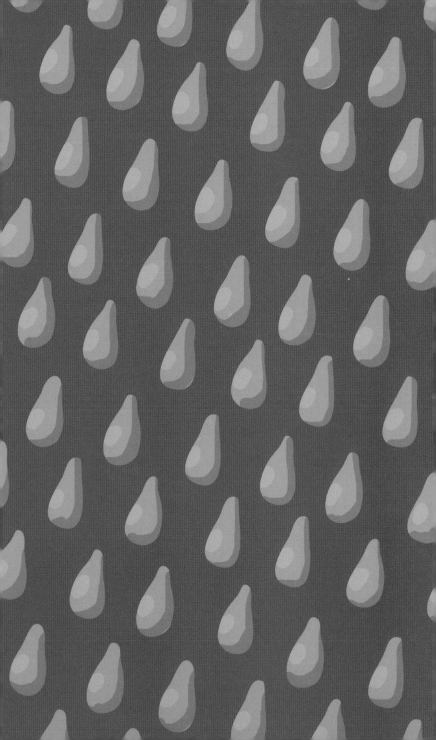

snow
---
nieve

(nee-eh-vay)

$$\frac{\text{sun}}{\text{sol}}$$

(sol)

tree

árbol

(ahr-bol)

flower
flor
(flor)

cake

---

pastel

(pas-tel)

cherry
cereza
(seh-reh-sa)

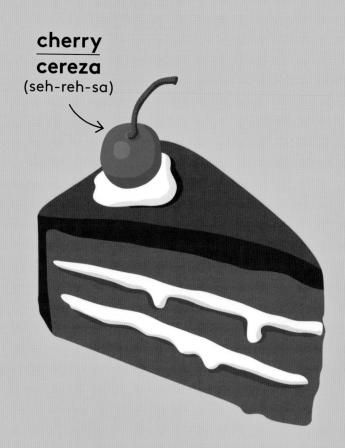

ball
---
pelota

(peh-lo-ta)

bird

pájaro

(pa-kha-roh)

egg
huevo
(way-voh)

umbrella

paraguas

(pa-ra-gwas)

rabbit
---
conejo
(ko-neh-khoh)

money
dinero

(dee-nair-roh)

bank
banco

(ban-koh)

mouse
ratón
(ra-ton)

scarf
bufanda

(boo-fan-da)

gloves

guantes

(gwan-tes)

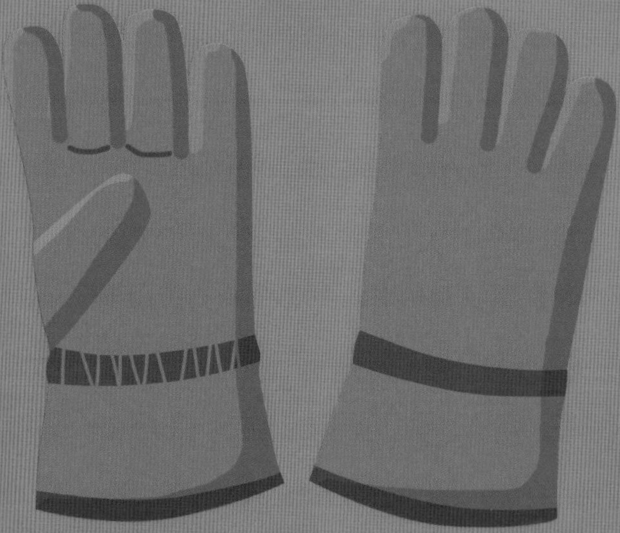

coat
---
abrigo

(a-bree-goh)

hospital
hospital
(os-pee-tal)

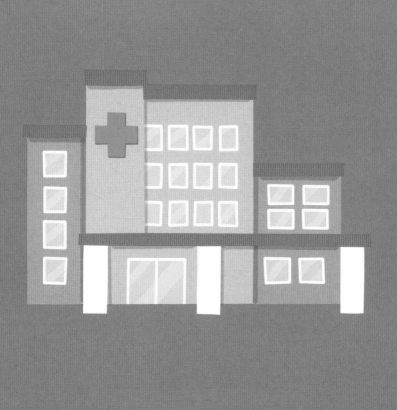

chair

---

silla

(see-lya)

table
---
mesa

(meh-sa)

toothbrush
cepillo de dientes
(theh-pee-lyo dey dyen-tes)

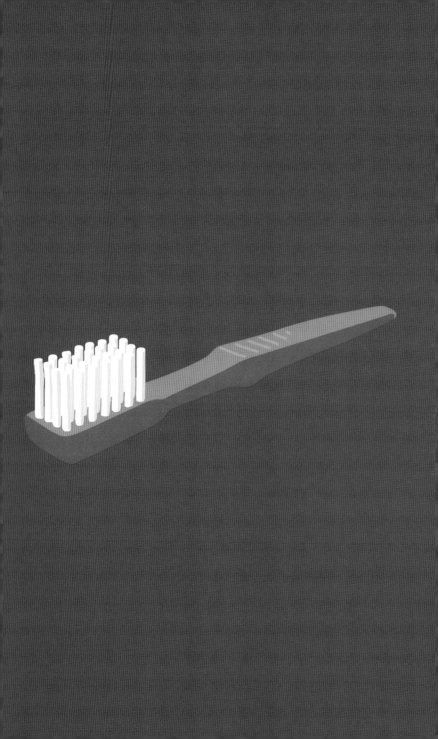

toothpaste
dentífrico

(den-tee-free-koh)

sun cream

---

crema solar

(kray-ma so-lar)

lion

---

león

(lay-on)

elephant
elefante
(eh-lay-fan-tay)

$$\frac{monkey}{mono}$$

(mo-noh)

spider

araña

(a-ra-nya)

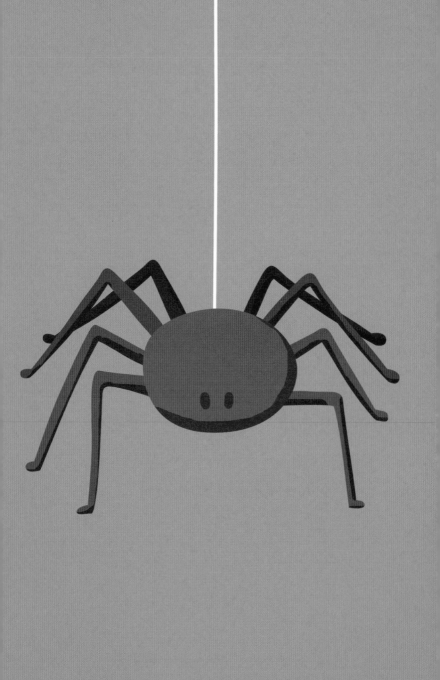

burger
hamburguesa

(am-boor-gay-sa)

pen

bolígrafo

(boh-lee-gra-foh)

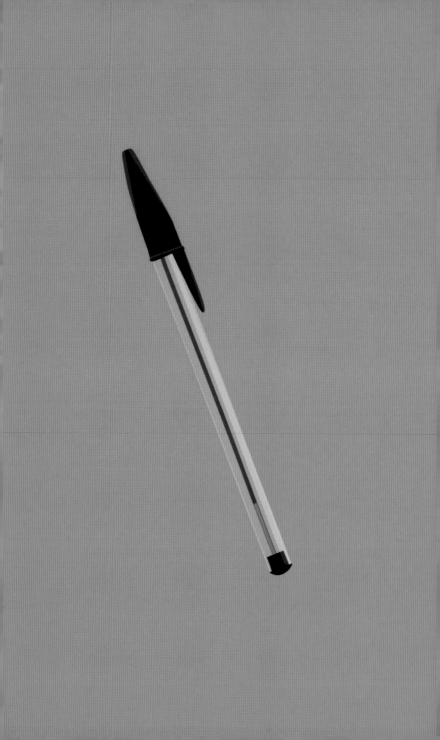

door
---
puerta
(pwair-ta)

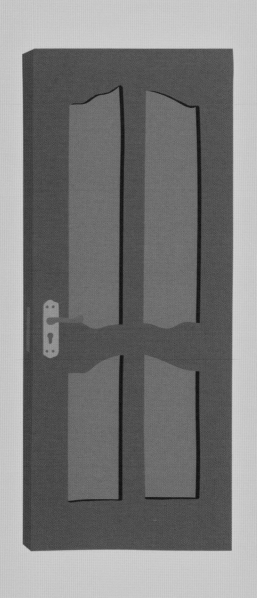

window
---
ventana

(ven-ta-na)

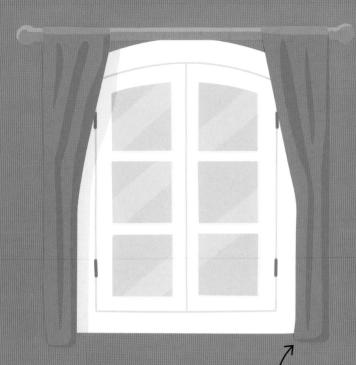

curtain

cortina

(cor-tee-na)

tent

tienda

(tee-en-da)

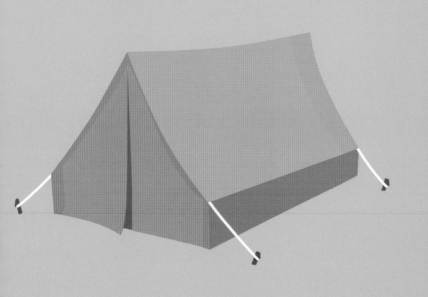

church
iglesia
(ee-glay-see-ah)

$$\frac{tomato}{tomate}$$

(tom-ah-tay)

moon
---
luna

(loo-na)

stars
estrellas
(es-tray-yas)

postcard
postal

(pos-tal)

stamp

sello

(say-yo)

boat
---
barco

(bar-koh)

goodbye / adiós

(a-dee-oss)